SUPER SHARKS

WHALE SHARK

Dan Lopez

Norwood House Press

Cataloging-in-Publication Data

Names: Lopez, Dan.
Title: Whale shark / Dan Lopez.
Description: Buffalo, NY : Norwood House Press, 2027. | Series: Super sharks | Includes glossary and index.
Identifiers: ISBN 9781978581463 (pbk.) | ISBN 9781978581470 (library bound) | ISBN 9781978581487 (ebook)
Subjects: LCSH: Whale shark--Juvenile literature.
Classification: LCC QL638.95.R4 L67 2027 | DDC 597.3--dc23

Published in 2027 by
Norwood House Press
2544 Clinton Street
Buffalo, NY 14224

Designer: Rhea Magaro
Editor: Tricia Hoffman

Photo credits: Cover, p. 1 Subphoto.com/Shutterstock.com; p. 4 Jellyman Photography/Shutterstock.com; p. 5 Iwan_Rusly/Shutterstock.com; p. 6 Leith Holtzman/Shutterstock.com; p. 9 Tararat Tienpajeekul/Shutterstock.com; p. 10 Travel Tips and Stories/Shutterstock.com; p. 12 Lewis Burnett/Shutterstock.com; p. 13 Peter116/Shutterstock.com; p. 15 Fata Morgana by Andrew Marriott/Shutterstock.com; p. 16 Alex Rush/Shutterstock.com; p. 17 Rich Carey/Shutterstock.com; p. 18 Divefriday/Shutterstock.com; p. 21 Jona Sanchez/Shutterstock.com;

Printed in the United States of America

TABLE OF CONTENTS

What Is Special about Whale Sharks?

Whale sharks are not whales, but they are just as big! After blue whales and fin whales, they are the third largest creatures in the ocean.

These giants are gentle. They do not threaten people.

What Do Whale Sharks Look Like?

A whale shark is the world's largest fish. It is as big as a school bus!

Whale sharks can be more than 40 feet (12 meters) long. They can weigh 40,000 pounds (18,000 kilograms).

A whale shark has two **dorsal fins**. It has five **gill slits** on each side of its head. Hard ridges called **keels** run down the length of its body.

Whale sharks have thick, rubbery skin. Their backs can be gray, brown, or blue. Their bellies are white. Each has a **unique** pattern of spots and stripes.

WHERE DO WHALE SHARKS LIVE?

Whale sharks swim slowly through **tropical** waters. They are found in the Atlantic, Pacific, and Indian oceans.

They are usually alone. Sometimes, they join **schools** that can have 100 whale sharks!

How Do Whale Sharks Hunt?

Whale sharks are **carnivores**, but they do not hunt. They are filter feeders. They swim with their mouths open to gulp seawater. The water flows through filter pads inside the shark's mouth. The pads have tiny holes that act like **sieves** to catch food. Water exits through the gill slits.

A whale shark eats thousands of pounds of **plankton** each day. It also feeds on shrimp, small fish, and **algae**.

When a whale shark finds a school of fish, it "stands" underneath. It opens and closes its huge mouth to create suction that pulls in lots of water—and lots of fish!

Remoras cling to whale sharks. The fish help keep the shark clean while they eat its scraps.

How Do Whale Sharks Reproduce?

Usually, about 16 live babies are born at one time, but it is possible for many more. They care for themselves as soon as they are born.

GLOSSARY

algae (AL-jee): small plants without roots or stems that grow mainly in water

carnivores (KAHR-nuh-vorz): animals that eat other animals

dorsal fins (DOR-sl finz): flat, thin body parts that stick up from the back of a shark or other marine animal

gill slits (gil slitz): openings on each side of a fish's head; where water exits after passing over the gills

keels (keelz): long, hard structures on a marine animal's body that work like a boat's keel to keep the animal upright in the water

plankton (PLANGK-tuhn): tiny animals that float and drift in the ocean

schools (skoolz): groups made up of many members of one fish species that swim together in a coordinated way

sieves (sivz): net-like containers that separate liquids from solids

tropical (TRAH-pi-kuhl): related to parts of Earth that are always hot and rainy

unique (yoo-NEEK): one of a kind; different from all others

Thinking Questions

1. How does a whale shark use its gill slits?
2. Describe a whale shark's coloring.
3. Where are whale sharks found on Earth?
4. Describe filter feeding.
5. What do whale sharks eat?

Index

About the Author

Dan Lopez lives far from the ocean in Indianapolis, Indiana, with his wife and three kids. He is fascinated by all of Earth's animals, including sharks! He admires their sleekness and speed and thinks more people should appreciate them.